Made in United States
Orlando, FL
05 February 2024

43288373R00067